Bio-Time's Impact on Living, Relationships & Sex

by

Henry H. Bowens

ISBN: 0-7596-4969-3

This book is printed on acid free paper.

1stBooks – rev. 4/25/02

Contents

Chapter 1

Introduction

You have acquired the opportunity to access the natural rhythm of sex, and the access to managing the influences of sex on personal behavior, relationships and daily living. Available for discovery and utilization are pleasure maximization of personal sexual experiences, greater access to romance, more effective management of finances, maximizing the benefits of diet and fitness programs, effective management of existing intimate relationships, increasing dating success rate, managing fidelity, and possible gender determination of children.

Note: *Personal benefits are available to the degree you participate in the exercises and use the included worksheets. However, you will greatly benefit even if you choose not to participate in the exercises, but you will not receive all that is available for you.*

<u>Bio-time</u>

All species of life are programmed to propagate. Propagation or the ability to bring forth life is a primary characteristic of that which is referred to as life or living. The propagation of many species is in accordance with the seasons or other natural rhythms that best ensure the survival of the offspring, and thus the species. Seasons and other natural rhythms are phases and/or periods, and thus are facets of time. Propagation is the primary means in which a species' survival is ensured. As such, propagation and the time to propagate, "bio-time" or biological clock, are not left to the discretion of individual members of the species. Instead, propagation is preprogrammed within each normal individual member of the species and is independent of the discretion of the individual members. In other words, the individual members do not truly have a say in the matter of propagation or the time of propagation.

Bio-time as referenced here is used to designate the natural timing of the reproductive cycles of the human species. Another reference for bio-time that is used in this text is the "peak sex period." The peak reproductive cycle is distinguished here as the period during the year when the male and female are naturally brought or pulled together for the sole purpose of propagation. The peak sex period is the same period and functions with the sometimes added or substituted purposes of pleasure maximization and ego fulfillment.

The human ego does not readily allow for that over which it has no control. Therefore, a peak sex period is out of the question for most of us, since we have no control over such phenomena. We, for the most part, consider ourselves to be equally sexually active throughout the entire year or all the time, and consider ourselves to be in full control of our sexual activity. Nothing could be farther from the truth. We, like many other species, have a period during respective individual twelve-month cycles when the desire to reproduce or participate in sexual activity is greater than any other time. In addition, we are not in control of it.

<u>Romanticism</u>

There is an explanation for this confusion over whether or not most of us actually experience a rise and fall in intensity of desire to be sexually active. We are, for the most part, romantics. Romanticism is held in high regard in our society, and individuals are made to feel bad, wrong or somehow inadequate if they are not romantic. Few of us have taken the time to look up the definition of romance and romanticism in the dictionary. The dictionary definition may be a big surprise to many of us. According to the dictionary, to be a romantic is "to exaggerate or invent detail or incident; or sympathetic imagination."

To be a romantic is to live in an unreal world; that is, a world that is an exaggeration, a world that is invented, or a world that is imagined. For example:

1) We romanticize that our sexual desire is the same throughout the year; perhaps because it is a validation of self-worth simply to think so.

2) We romanticize that we have control over our sexual desire, as well as when and with whom we happen to have sex.

3) We have virtually nothing to say about our sexual desire and we romanticize that we have total say about it.

4) We participate in the activities of reproduction because it is a natural irresistible mandate to do so, and we romanticize that we are at choice in the matter.

In regards to sex and relationships, we live in an unreal world or a world of fantasy, and do not know it. It is this unreal world undistinguished that is at the source of many female/male relationship dilemmas. This dialogue is not intended to label romance bad or an undesirable practice. Romance adds color to living life, and thus is very desirable. Problems arise when we forget we are romanticizing, and consider all that is romanticized to be real. For example:

1) We romanticize that our romantic partner loves us because of the great feelings, when these seemingly feelings of love are produced by bodily chemicals.

2) We romanticize that our romantic partner will be with us forever, when our partner cannot keep her/his word to fulfill on the simplest of promises.

In regards to sex, romance is simply a process of adding color and entertainment to that which is going to happen anyway, over and over and so on. The interesting thing is that most of us unknowingly refer to this added color as "Love" and consider ourselves to be "in Love."

<u>Sex</u>

It is no secret that sexual desire impacts our actions and behavior, and thus our whole life. It impacts all of our relationships and associations with other people, financial well-being, mental and emotional well-being, physical well-being, family, businesses, communities, social activities, government, entertainment, and so on. There is hardly an area of life that sexual desire does not influence. Sex is one of the most reliable human physical experiences for generating great sensual sensations of euphoria and pleasure. It is for this reason that many businesses associate their products with the sexual experience. When businesses do this we are naturally drawn to the products, have good feelings towards the products, buy the products and tell others about our experience of the product. The good feelings we associate with the products are merely sexual stimulation, and the good feelings have nothing to do with the products themselves. It is true, "sex sells."

Many of us, when not under the influence of romanticism, have consciously experienced rises and falls in our sexual desire. The rises and falls have been attributed to many things except the true nature of sexual desire itself. The wisest of us have discovered the basic secret to what many refer to as the key to great sex, which is "when you are hot, you are hot, and when you are not, you are not." The source of confusion in this area is our romanticizing of specific individuals, events, circumstances or places as the cause of us being "hot" or "not hot." The good news is that sexual desire has everything to do with you and little or nothing to do with someone or something else. The bad news is that from this point forward you will no longer get to blame someone or something else because you are not sexually turned on.

Time

Many of us really see that sex is only as great as we are "hot" or horny. The mystery has been **"When are you hot and not hot?"** Time or "when" is the missing dimension in our endeavors to manage our sexual activity and the resultant outcomes of sex. The dimension of time transforms our rather gray, uncontrollable or muddy relationship with sex to the clarity of simply black or white. In other words, the seasons of sex that were once invisible are now visible. This newfound ability to distinguish the seasons of sex grants, for the first time, the opportunity to control and manage the effects of sex.

The basic principle underlying bio-time was discovered more than twenty-five years ago, and has been observed and studied operating in the lives of hundreds of individuals and families over this period. Bio-time has been consistently seventy to eighty percent accurate in predicting the impact of changes in sexual desire on individual behavior. This is extraordinary given that it operates in an environment of other natural and synthetic sexual stimulants and depressants. Large amounts of data from scientific studies are not presented here to convince you that bio-time is viable. Bio-time's validity cannot personally be seen or validated in that manner. Instead, worksheets and a bio-time or "peak sex period" calendar have been included for your use, so that you have an opportunity to generate a personal experience of its validity and utility. Personal experiences are more valid and useful than personal beliefs and concepts. Thus, the goal here is not to have you believe in bio-time but to have you experience it. The personal experience will permit you to observe it operating in the lives of friends, associates, relatives and other families, as well as grant you a new level of mastery in effectively managing intimate relationships.

Henry H. Bowens

Chapter 2

How Bio-Time Works

The underlying operating principle of **bio-time, peak sex period,** is simply this: Each of us is naturally out to recreate or reproduce our respective birthday through prospective offspring. That is; if you were born on January 1, you are naturally out to have children that are born on January 1; if you were born on March 16, you are naturally out to have children that are born on March 16; if you were born on October 28, you are naturally out to have children that are born on October 28; and so on. To recreate your birthday, the best time for child conception is naturally set at ninety days after your birthday. This naturally factors in the nine months incubation period of the human fetus. Thus, your greatest desire to participate in sexual activity occurs ninety days following your birthday.

[Before you say, "got you, I was not born on the birthday of my parents nor do I know anyone that was born on the birthday of their parents," stay with me a little longer.]

The day of greatest sexual desire occurs ninety days after the birthday. Sexual desire starts to gradually build with the ocurrence of the birthday and gradually increases to the ninetieth day peak, and gradually declines at the same rate for the following ninety days. A graphical representation of the increase and decrease in sexual desire is depicted below.

90 Days

An individual's **natural** sexual activity, if not influenced in any fashion, follows the gradual rise and fall of their sexual desire. This excludes influences such as seduction by another in their peak sex period, prostitution, other synthetic influences, or circumstances that increase or decrease sexual activity. Naturally occurring sexual activity follows the cyclical nature of sexual desire, or the increases and decreases in sex hormone levels.

Since sexual activity increases with increases in sexual desire, the likelihood of conception increases also because of the increase in sexual activity. Thus, it is more likely that children will not be born on the exact birthday of their parents because conception is likely to occur before the peak. Other personal, psychological, physical, social, economic and/or environmental factors are likely to prevent sex and conception from occurring on the day which might result in the exact duplication of a parent's birthday. Another factor that influences the duplication of a parent's birthday is that the female and male do not normally have the same birthday. As a result, their peak periods are not the same, and both are not "hot" at the same time. Thus, if one desires sex, the other may not; and this prevents either birthday from being duplicated, except in rare instances. In the more male dominated cultures, sexual activity coincides more with the sexual desires of the male. The evidence is the clustering of the offspring or children around the father's birthday as opposed to that of the mother's. To discover which of one's parents was dominant in fulfilling her/his sexual desire, all one has to do is observe which parent the children's birthdays most cluster around.

Chapter 3

The Peak Sex Period Calendar

This is an opportunity to validate the viability of the peak sex period through your and others' personal experiences and history. Take the opportunity to play with or use the worksheets that are included. Doing so will handle most, if not all, skepticism you might have.

As previously mentioned, a Peak Sex Period Calendar has been included for convenience. The calendar months of the year, representing the peak sex periods, are listed horizontally across the top of the **Calendar**. The first six months of the year are repeated so that the peak sex periods are contained linearly on a single page. This makes it easier to compare the peak sex periods of different individuals. The birthday of the individual is represented by the calendar months of the year listed vertically in the first column of the **Calendar**.

The **Calendar's** peak sex period has been divided into seven distinct periods or calendar months. These periods are represented by color or shaded bars. There is a color bar for each period or month within the peak sex period. Each color bar represents approximately thirty days. There are four distinct colors or shading gradients. The color or shading coded "Highest" is the period representing the ninety days after the birthday, which is the period of highest sexual desire. The color or shading coded "Low" represents the start and end of the relevant period of peak sexual desire. The color shadings coded "Moderate" and "High" represent the increasing sexual desire towards the peak and the declining sexual desire after the peak.

To determine your period of peak sexual desire simply move down the first column to locate your month of birth and move horizontally across to the shaded or color bars.

The months above included in your bar make up your peak period of sexual desire. If your birthday falls in the second half of the month, a more accurate presentation of your peak sex period would be that of the following month. For example, if your birthday is April 16 or later, May would best reflect the beginning of your peak sex period. If

PEAK SEX PERIOD CALENDAR

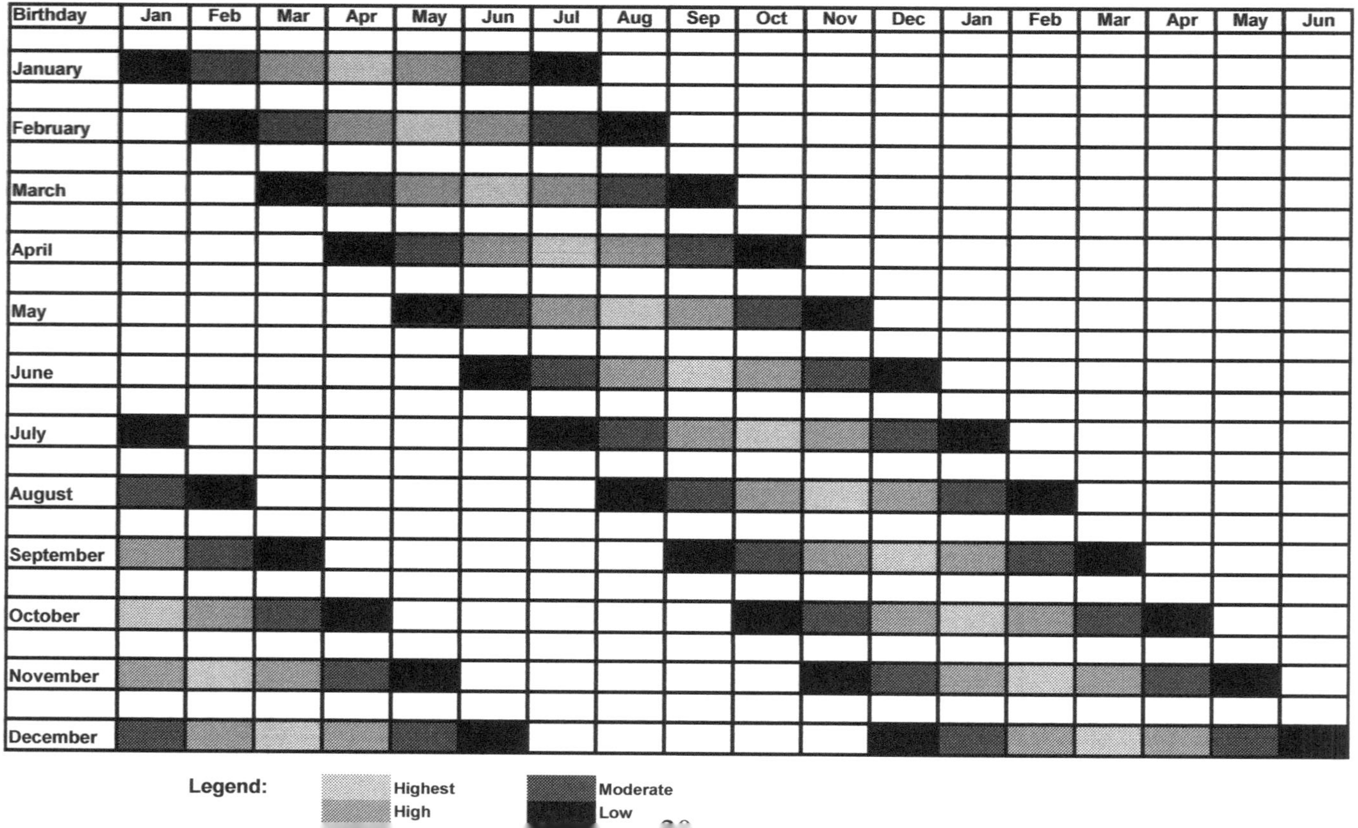

Birthday	Jan	Feb	Mar	Apr	May	Jun	Jul	Aug	Sep	Oct	Nov	Dec	Jan	Feb	Mar	Apr	May	Jun
January																		
February																		
March																		
April																		
May																		
June																		
July																		
August																		
September																		
October																		
November																		
December																		

Legend:

- Highest
- High
- Moderate
- Low

you would like an accurate portrayal of your peak sex period, simply count out thirty, sixty, ninety, one-hundred twenty, one-hundred fifty and one-hundred eighty days from your birthday and note these on **Worksheet A**. At the beginning of your period your birthday will be the "Low" period, the thirty-day point will be your "Moderate" period, the sixty-day point will be your "High" period, and the ninety-day point will be your "Highest" period. For the second half of your period the one hundred-twenty day point is the "High" period, the one hundred-fifty day point is the "Moderate" period and the one hundred-eighty day point is the "Low" period. All that is needed to determine anyone's peak period of sexual desire is her/his birthday.

Exercise: Gather the birthdays of your parents and your siblings, if you have any, and write their day and month of birth in the spaces contained on **Worksheet B**. **Worksheet B** depicts the peak sex period of your parents. You will likely discover that you and your siblings were conceived during the peak sex period of one or both of your parents, with few and rare exceptions. Enter your father's and mother's birthday and month under the respective column designated for them. Enter your and your siblings' day and month of birth next to the parent that they were born nearest.

> 1) Note whether you and your siblings were born within three months of either parent's birthday.

PEAK SEX PERIOD
Worksheet A

LOW	MODERATE	HIGH	HIGHEST	HIGH	MODERATE	LOW

2) Note if you and your siblings were born within two months or one month of either parent's birthday.

3) Note if either of you were born in the same month of either parent's birthday.

4) Note if you or one of your siblings were born on the same day as one of your parents.

The parent with the most kids clustering around their birth month was the hottest, most sexually influential or had the most intense sexual desire during their peak sex period. It is recommended that you repeat this process with several other families to further ascertain that children are conceived primarily during the peak sex period of one or the other parent.

You now know when mom and dad are hot and when they are not. If your parents' peak sex periods are near each other or the same, then your father is likely to be the one who is sexually dominant or hottest if you and most of your siblings are male. Study observations have shown that most males are conceived during the peak sex period of the father and most females are conceived during the peak sex period of the mother. Thus, your mother is likely to be the sexually hottest if you and your siblings are mostly female. If the sex of the kids is evenly distributed, both parents are equally sexually influential. Plot the birth data of the families of relatives and friends, and observe the extent to which males are conceived during the peak sex period of the father and the extent to which females are conceived during the peak sex period of the mother. How and why this happens will be discussed later.

There are children that are conceived outside of their parents' peak sex periods; however, these occurrences are few relative to those that are conceived inside the parents' peak sex periods. As mentioned earlier, humans are sexual year round, which makes conception outside of the peak sex period likely. The incidence of conception increases with sexual activity. Sexual activity increases with increases in sexual desire. Sexual desire increases in the peak sex period.

PEAK SEX PERIOD
Worksheet B

Sibling Name	Sibling Birthday			Father's Birthday	Sibling Birthday		
	Three Months Prior	Two Months Prior	One Month Prior		One Month After	Two Months After	Three Months After

Sibling Name	Sibling Birthday			Mother's Birthday	Sibling Birthday		
	Three Months Prior	Two Months Prior	One Month Prior		One Month After	Two Months After	Three Months After

Worksheet A can also be used to monitor and log your past and current activities during your peak sex period. Write in events and activities in the periods they happened. Some examples are an increased interest in a mate, the opposite sex becoming more attractive, an increased desire to be more social, an increased interest in your physical appearance expressed as new clothing, dieting and physical exercise, a first date with a special person, a first kiss and/or sexual encounter with a special person, the purchase of a home and/or durable goods, and relationship issues and breakups.

The more past experiences you are able to log the more insight you will gain into the effects of bio-time on you and others. It is oftentimes easier to see the effects of the cyclical nature of sex on others. Thus, it would be

PEAK SEX PERIOD
Worksheet C

Child Name	Child Birthday			Your Birthday	Child Birthday		
	Three Months Prior	Two Months Prior	One Month Prior		One Month After	Two Months After	Three Months After

Child Name	Child Birthday			Spouse Birthday	Child Birthday		
	Three Months Prior	Two Months Prior	One Month Prior		One Month After	Two Months After	Three Months After

very valuable for you to observe and log the behavior and activities of others as they move through their respective peak sex periods. This will allow you to see the effects on you a lot clearer.

Worksheet C is included for logging your family's birth data if you are a parent, and it may also be used for other families. **Worksheet D** is included to be used to log the peak sex periods of family members and friends so that you can see the effects of the peak sex period on them.

PEAK SEX PERIOD
Worksheet D

Name	Birthday	DAY and MONTH						
		LOW	MODERATE	HIGH	HIGHEST	HIGH	MODERATE	LOW

Chapter 4

Symptoms of the Peak Sex Period

The opportunity of this chapter is to become familiar with the effects of the peak sex period on your and others' behavior. This will grant you greater access to managing the effects of the peak sex period. In addition to healthy fertile individuals, these symptoms have been observed in individuals who are beyond their child bearing years, who are impotent, and who have had reproductive organs surgically removed.

There are behavioral changes when you start your "low" period of the peak sex period. You start to become more interested in your physical appearance. This is often expressed as starting diets in order to lose weight; beginning physical exercise programs to tone up muscles and reshape the body, and/or increase physical stamina; shopping for new clothing; buying and wearing clothing that accentuates you sexually; and/or shifting your preference for colors from relatively conservative to non-conservative, such as moving from grays and dull color shades to colors in the red family or bright colors. If you take vacations, they will likely be unconsciously planned to coincide with the highest period of your peak sex period. If you purchase a car during this period you are likely to select red or another color that expresses your sexuality. You begin to be interested in being more sexually attractive. All of this occurs naturally without you being conscious of what is driving your actions and activities. Notice that the emphasis here is to be more attractive and physically fit. This is naturally done in preparation for the highest period of the peak sex period where the height of sexual desire is fulfilled by the height of sexual activity. Increased physical stamina is needed to satisfy the physical demands of the coming heightened sexual activity.

On the domestic front during the "low" period: You will likely become interested in buying a home or a new home, interested in home improvements and repairs, interested in redecorating an existing home, and/or interested in the acquisition of new furnishings for the home. This is the naturally occurring management of the "nest" given by this heightened reproductive cycle. You are naturally and unconsciously driven to prepare for the arrival of new offspring. Because this is happening naturally without you having anything to say about it, you justify your actions by saying something like, "I am just tired of the old and want something new."

Also, it is likely that you will become critical of your mate's physical appearance if your mate is overweight and/or critical of the clothing your mate wears. The male that is more physically fit, well dressed or groomed and prosperous will be found to be more attractive by the female. The female fat that is properly accentuated, promoting the bodily curves, will be very attractive to the male; because his subconscious naturally occurring theme is "there is plenty of baby food here."

Moderate and High Periods

Upon entering the "moderate" and "high" periods of the peak sex period, you will likely experience an increased desire to participate in various social events or the area's nightlife. The increased desire to be more socially active is the result of you naturally seeking a mate. Thus, you will place yourself where you might be discovered for the purpose of mating.

You are likely to make high dollar purchases in the areas of clothing, vehicles, houses and/or household furnishings and durable goods. This could occur in the "low" period as well. You naturally use items such as clothing and vehicles to enhance your personal esteem, and to appear more attractive and available to a prospective mate. Your renewed interest in your dwelling is the result of you naturally desiring a suitable place, nest, to raise prospective children.

The Highest Period

In the "highest" period you are driven to participate in sex to the point of being stupid or unreasonable. This is the period in which most people have their experiences of great sex or the best sex ever. All you can seem to think about is sex. You are likely to be swept away by anything that is sexually stimulating, including your sexual partner. The unconscious natural goal here is conception. The more often sexual intercourse occurs, the better chance of conception. Propagation is happening and "Human Species" is very pleased.

After the Highest Period

The "high" and "moderate" periods following the "highest" is where you are likely to conclude that you have found the one you have been looking or waiting for, the person you are with is close enough to your ultimate fantasy partner, or you are "IN LOVE." You will likely establish yourselves as a couple. You are likely to get engaged or even married. Most engagements and/or marriages occur during the peak sex period of one or the other partner. If you are single and are committed to remaining that way, look out and be very careful during this period. It does not matter if it is not your peak sex period. The influence of your partner during this period may be great enough to have you do anything they desire. Given your romanticism, you will invent or imagine your partner to be deeply in love with you. In reality, it has nothing much to do with you, it is all about propagation.

After the Peak Sex Period

The following "low" period and the period afterward are likely to present some surprises to you. Once you and your partner are no longer under the influence of the strong sexual desire, you may find yourselves not very related. You are likely to be more critical of each other and even argue about things you would have never considered arguing about. You will likely question any engagement plans you have made together, wonder how you ever got related to this person, or wake up and wonder how you ended up married to the person next to you. It is like you have been in a trance and are now waking up to find all the things you have gotten yourself into. If the truth be told, you have been in a trance.

The increased sexual desire alters reality for us. Things or people that were not attractive become attractive and we end up doing or committing to things we normally would not do or commit to. When the sexual desire shifts back to normal or manageable levels, our perception of reality reverts back as well.

You may find yourself bored or mildly depressed since you are no longer being driven by the strong sexual desire of your peak sex period. You will likely blame this on your partner. You will accuse her/him of not turning you on anymore and not loving you. You will think the missing fire or chemistry is her/his fault. You may go as far as ending the relationship in the hopes of finding someone else who will "light your fire." This will likely be your attempt to deal with the boredom and mild depression. It is during this period of reduced sexual desire that relationships end. What you were experiencing during the period of peak sexual desire is a natural phenomenon that you have very little to say about. Given that you were totally unaware of the peak sex period, you did not even have the smallest say in the matter of your sexual activity. The bottom line here is that you do not have to kill off your partner and/or trade her/him for another one. There is nothing wrong with you or her/him. Your sexual desire is cyclical. Your season will come again. **<u>You will be hot again!</u>**

The mild depression at the end of your peak sex period is the result of a change in your body chemistry. Your body is producing fewer sexual chemicals or hormones and you have not yet adapted to the reduction. Attempts to compensate for the chemical reduction by ingesting stimulants is common. An increase in the consumption of stimulants such as alcohol, tobacco or other drugs is likely, if these substances are already a part of your diet. Food is also a stimulant and chances are your consumption of it will increase. Foods containing sugar, chocolate and caffeine will likely be consumed in larger quantities. This is the period in which unhealthy eating and exercise habits are likely to start. Understanding this period and how it affects you will allow you to avoid the unhealthy pitfalls that arise during this period. The time required for you to adjust to the lower level of natural stimulants or sexual chemicals is just a matter of weeks. So, become familiar with this period and how it affects you. Doing so will permit you to successfully navigate this period with few problems and interruptions in your health routines.

Tip: To become familiar with how the peak sex period affects your behavior and activities specifically, keep a personal journal beginning with your birthday through the end of your peak sex period. Maintaining a personal journal will assist you in being conscious throughout your peak sex period. Without a journal or a personal reminder, you will be so caught up in the effects of your peak sex period that you will forget such a thing exists.

Chapter 5

Peak Sex Period Benefits and Uses

The benefits and uses of the peak sex period technology are presented in this chapter. The benefits and uses that will be discussed are by no means all that are possible. As you play with and practice this technology, you will discover new uses and possibilities for it. The intent here is to provide immediate utility of the technology so that you immediately experience personal value. Have fun with the technology and do not use it in the disservice of others.

<u>Family Planning</u>

First: Couples or individuals desiring to have children can determine when during the year conception is most likely to occur. Conception is more likely to occur during their respective peak sex periods and extremely likely if both share the same or similar period. This enables couples or individuals to focus efforts to conceive children during the periods when children are most likely to be conceived. This saves time, money, and the mental stress that usually follow failed attempts to get pregnant during the non-peak sex periods.

Second: Couples or individuals desiring not to have children can better manage contraceptives and other methods and techniques to prevent pregnancy. The peak sex periods are the periods of the year to be the most cautious.

Third: It is possible to determine the sex of a desired child. As previously mentioned, females are conceived, for the most part, during the peak sex period of the mother, and males are most often conceived during the peak sex period of the father. A number of things can account for this. The first is that the female vaginal discharge is likely to be heavier during the female's peak sex period. The vaginal discharge is harmful to the male chromosome-carrying sperm. Medical researchers have demonstrated that the chemical makeup of the female reproductive area is least favorable to male chromosome-carrying sperm during a time of the year that, incidentally, coincides with the female peak sex period. A chemically unfavorable environment for the male chromosome-carrying sperm reduces the likelihood of a male child being conceived. Second, the male in his peak sex period may be less prone to engaging in foreplay with the female or properly preparing her for sex. The female's role is now one of accommodating her partner and her vaginal fluid is at its minimal level, which is a more favorable environment for the male chromosome-carrying sperm. Additionally, it is also more likely that the male sperm count is lower in off-peak sex periods and higher during the male's peak sex period. However, though both male and female are involved in determining the sex of a child, the female is the final determinant of the child's sex. If the female enjoys and/or loves sex, chances are the resulting child will be female. If she does not, chances are the resulting child will be male. If the desired gender of the prospective child is to be female, ensure the mother-to-be is in her peak sex period, ensure she is properly prepared for sex via sexual foreplay, and ensure and be attentive that she finds the sexual experience pleasurable. If a male child is desired, a simple **"wham bam thank you ma'am"** will do the trick.

During a coaching session with a client in which the influences of the peak sex period were being distinguished in his current relationship, the client suddenly became puzzled. He shared with me that his father was born in December and his mother was born in October. He and his two brothers were born in November, and he had a younger sister, supposedly an accident, born in September. He was clear that he and his siblings had been conceived during his parents' peak sex period. His question was, "Why were there three boys and only one girl, the accident?" Since his mother was in her peak sex period during each child conception, it was reasonable to assume that more of the children should have been female. Upon closer examination of his parents' relationship, it was discovered that they were engaged in planned pregnancy. He and his two brothers were planned and his younger sister was not. His parents' objective was to simply cause pregnancy. They were out to get the sperm to the egg in the fastest and most effective means possible. To this end, sexual foreplay and pleasure were not viable and meaningful parts of their plan. The fulfillment of the plan resulted in male children. After his parents had their desired number of children, they later found themselves just fooling around and having fun with sex during their peak sex periods. The resultant child was his sister, the accident. He now saw more clearly that female sexual pleasure most often results in female children.

New Parenting Tool

First: Parents that have kids of dating age can predict when during the year their kids will more likely engage in sexual activities. This allows the parents to adjust their kids' activities and manage the conditions that are conducive for sex to occur, based on the preferences of the parents.

Second: Parents have access to knowing the peak sex period of other kids that their kids are dating or participating with socially. This allows the parent to manage the influence of others or peer pressure on their kids to engage in sexual activities. Kids are more prone to getting into trouble during their peak sex period as a result of the increased desire to participate in social activities. Since it can be readily determined when kids will be more socially active and more likely to participate in sexual activities, parents know when to concentrate efforts on minimizing their kids' undesirable activities and outcomes. Minimizing the undesirable activities and outcomes is achieved by managing the type and/or amount of the kids' social activities during their peak sex period.

Relationship Gossip

First: You can observe who is likely to be the sexually dominant person in a marriage or relationship simply by noting when the children were born. If the conception occurred during the female's peak sex period, you will know that it is the female who is likely running the sexual show. The male is dominating the bedroom if the children are clustered around his birthday. If the children are equally or near equally clustered around both their birthdays, there is generous give and take in the relationship. To say it differently, they generously listen to and support each other.

Second: You can tell if the woman in the relationship is enjoying the sex by the gender of the children. In families in which the children are all female, the woman is definitely enjoying the sex and/or calling the shots when it comes to sex, and/or her mate is a great lover. In families in which the children are all male, the woman is not likely enjoying the sex and her mate dominates the bedroom, and/or her mate is a terrible lover. The men who claim to be great lovers are likely liars if their offspring are all male, and their mates' orgasms are likely to be fakes.

<u>Dating</u>

First: If you are just out to have sex, your chances of success are high if your prospective partner is in her/his peak sex period. You can now determine if they are in their peak sex period by asking a very innocent and simple question, "When is your birthday?"

Second: If you have been out to date and/or seduce someone specifically and she/he has been unreceptive, your chances of success improve as she/he enters her/his peak sex period. Sexually cold or inactive individuals have no choice but to heat up or become more open to dating and/or sex during their respective peak sex periods. It is advisable to start the courtship as close to her/his peak sex period as possible to beat out other persons who might be interested.

Birthday gifts given to her/him will likely be perceived as being very romantic, and will have her/him start to have romantic fantasies about you. Gifts are effective romantic gestures primarily during the receiver's peak sex period and are rarely perceived as romantic during the receiver's non-peak sex period. In order to get the most mileage from gifts in terms of romance, give them during the receiver's peak sex period. It is natural for you to give gifts when you are in the first phase of your peak sex period, and they occur for you as romantic gestures or great expressions of your deepest emotions. However, as aforementioned, gifts are not likely to be perceived as being romantic by the receiver unless the receiver is also in her/his peak sex period. So, do not be too disappointed if your gifts do not have your intended affect on the receiver. It is not the receiver's time to perceive your gifts as romantic if she/he is not in her/his peak sex period.

The birthday gift initiates all that is perceived to be romantic, loving and caring about you in the mind of the person with whom you are intimately related or your spouse. So, never forget and/or fail to give her/him a birthday gift on her/his birthday. Failure to do so will most likely result in the perception that you no longer care about and love her/him.

Third: If you have been out to have this very special person in your life commit to marriage or a more permanent relationship, approach the person during their peak sex period. Try the "low" period first. The instinct to nest may have them say "yes" to you. If they continue to hold out, approach them again during their "high" period following the "highest" period. The person's resistance will be at its lowest here and she/he will likely say "yes" to your request. A word of caution is needed here: You will have to rigorously manage the relationship once the person is out of their peak sex period because she/he will no longer be under the influence of her/his peak sex period.

Fourth: You have access to managing the degree of sexual passion in your relationship. To say it another way, you have access to determining whether you have great sex, good sex or okay sex. This is accomplished through access to the peak sex periods of prospective mates. Select a mate with the same or nearly the same peak sex period as yours, and you will both be insanely lustful at the same time. The sexual energy generated under this condition is exponential rather than linear, and it is very explosive. Caution should be exercised here because you will both be sexually cold at the same time, and this is a clearing for relationship issues and problems to arise, as previously discussed.

Selecting a mate whose peak sex period begins six months after yours ensures that one of you will be generating sexual passion when the other is not. This will have sexual passion in the relationship throughout the year. Okay sex is the likely outcome of this extreme and more sexual seduction of the mate not in her/his peak sex period is required. This can add fun and play to the relationship.

Selecting a mate between these two peak sex period extremes, great sex and okay sex, will result in varying degrees of good sex. The closer the respective peak sex periods the more intense the sexual energy. The further apart the respective peak sex periods, the less intense the sexual energy gets. You can dial in the desired degree of sexual energy in a relationship simply by the choice of a mate.

Physical Fitness

It is best to start physical fitness programs at the start of the peak sex period. The naturally occurring desire to be attractive will assist in establishing exercise as a permanent practice in your life. The duration of the peak sex period is sufficient enough to have your body become accustomed to and desire exercise.

Domestic Chores

You are likely to be successful in having your "honey-do-lists" completed during your mate's peak sex period. Your mate will be in her/his nesting phase and will work on and/or complete the projects with enthusiasm. She/he will be happy for the opportunity to get the nest in shape. Designating projects for this period will reduce arguments and other damaging conversations and moods that are detrimental to the relationship. If the projects are not managed such that they are completed within the peak sex period, chances are they will not be completed until the next peak sex period.

On the other side of the coin, you will know when to be on the lookout in regards to new projects. "Honey-do-lists" are more likely to be compiled during the peak sex period of your mate. The same natural desires that have you or her/him happy to complete such lists also gives rise to the lists.

Major Monetary Expenditures

The beginning of your mate's peak sex period is also the best time to have her/him agree to buying a new automobile, redecorating, remodeling and/or the purchase of a new home. Men are especially generous with their wealth or money in regards to their mate during their peak sex period. Many women resist the generous gestures of their mate during this period. It is advisable that women allow this full expression of male generosity to flow unabated, and manage or steer it in a direction that best supports the relationship or marriage.

Managing the Budget

Monetary expenditures are higher during the peak sex period. Besides the additional expenditures used for the nest or home, additional expenditures for social events, eating out, recreation, new clothing and new vehicles occur during this period. You are likely to wake up after this period and wonder how you got into all the new debt you have. The compulsion to spend money during the peak sex period is almost irresistible. This is a primary source of too much debt or unmanageable debt among individuals and couples. Understanding this allows for the effective management of the budget at the time when management is most needed, the peak sex period.

<u>Business</u>

There are business benefits to knowing your clients' peak sex period. If you are in the business of beauty consulting, real estate, home building, home improvements and repairs, automobile, furniture and appliances, and/or sell other durable goods for the home, you can determine the best time to call on clients for sales simply by knowing their birthdays. The clients' peak sex periods are the best time for sales calls. The non-peak sex period is the period in which clients are most likely rigorously managing debt from peak sex period expenditures. Clients that are rigorously managing debt are poor candidates for new sales. Thus, to maximize the dollars per unit of sales effort or be more effective at selling, call on clients when they are spending money and not managing debt.

<u>Managing the Relationship</u>

First: You have access to reducing relationship breakups, and minimizing conversations and actions that damage relationships. After the peak sex period is over, you and your mate have an opportunity to generate a relationship not based in lust. This will be easy to do because the lust or sexual desire is at a level that you both can manage. Remember, it is very easy to end the relationship because of a perception that something is wrong with you or your mate because of the diminished lust. You are both fine. You have ended one season and begun another. This is the period to get to know your mate mentally, emotionally and spiritually. You have mastered that which is physical about each other. This is the period to generate the other three dimensions of the relationship.

The end of the peak sex period is an opportunity to be truly related to your partner. During the peak sex period you are at the effect or driven by the strong chemical currents that make up sexual desire. Your experience of yourself and of others is shaped by sexual desire. The relationship is automatic, biological and requires no creative effort by you. When you cease to be at the effect of that which is driving you, boredom occurs. You likely relate to boredom as an awful and terrible thing, and try to get rid of it at all costs. However, boredom is a very high state of consciousness. Boredom means that you are no longer a slave to that which was driving you, and you are now your own master and are free to create. In regards to relationships, to be the master is to be willing to be the **cause or creator of your experience** of your partner. The relationship is present when each person in the relationship is creating her/his experience of the other. The freedom and opportunity to create your own experiences of another are more available when you are not at the effect of sexual desire.

Second: Infidelity is more likely to occur during your and others' peak sex period than any other period of the respective twelve-month cycles. Your mate, in her/his peak sex period, will find others sexually attractive and tempting. This does not mean that you are not sexy and attractive. Many of us indulge ourselves in the romantic fantasy that our partner finds only us sexually attractive. We even go as far as using this fantasy as the justification for our partner loving us and only us. However, nothing could be further from the truth in regards to sexual attraction. Sexual attraction does not discriminate or adhere to personal, racial, political or cultural boundaries. Sexual attraction is natural, automatic, and is beyond individual control or discretion. Sexual attraction is the natural means of distinguishing who is fertile, compatible and available for mating, and who is not. Sexual attraction is not "Love" and does not mean that we have to have the person or persons we find sexually attractive; this is simply the meaning we attach to sexual attraction.

The peak sex period is the period of greatest sexual attraction and desire, and the period of least personal control and discretion over sexual activity. If you have a cheating partner, you will likely uncover evidence of it during her/his peak sex period. If you are the one cheating, you will find others more sexually irresistible during your peak sex period. Additionally, other people in their peak sex period are more likely to seek out you or your mate, which presents added sexual temptation. It is not possible to manage sexual infidelity such that no infidelity will ever occur, if it is not your or your partner's will or commitment to maintain the fidelity of the relationship.

Tip: There are steps you can take to reduce the effects of sexual temptation from others on your mate. First Step: Make yourself sexually available to your mate during her/his peak sex period. This will require rigorous management if your peak sex period is near opposite to that of your mate's. The time to indulge in personal recreational activities and hobbies, such as golf, is during your mate's non-peak sex period. Your mate will likely want to see less of you during her/his non-peak sex period.

Second Step: Knowing the peak sex periods of your and your mate's associates, colleagues and friends allows you the wherewithal to manage the degree of sexual temptation you both might experience. This can be accomplished by managing the private access of others to you and your mate during the respective peak sex periods of others. This is especially necessary if their peak sex period coincides with yours and/or that of your mate's. Jealousy is how this is naturally managed, but jealousy often results in arguments or suppression of your and your mate's self-expression, which is detrimental to the relationship. So, consciously manage the fidelity and avoid the pitfalls of jealousy, the natural manager.

Chapter 6

Sexual Assault and the Peak Sex Period

The purpose of this chapter is to provide an actual illustration that validates the overpowering influence of sexual desire on the behavior and actions of individuals during their respective peak sex period. This illustration is also provided for the readers who did not take the time to ground themselves on the personal effects of the peak sex period via the use of the worksheets, and those that require an outside study rather than a personal illustration.

Sexual assault was selected as the illustration because of the overwhelming public concern and interest in sex crimes. The illustration is a study of individuals accused and convicted of sex crimes. The purpose of the study was to illuminate any correlation between the sex crimes and the respective peak sex periods of the offenders. The study was performed on a group of sex offenders in Texas. Since Texas is an open records state, there was no problem obtaining the needed data on the sex offenders to determine their peak sex periods and the dates of their respective crimes. The information source did not contain sufficient information to determine the peak sex periods of the victims.

The offenders were selected from an online source on a first-see first-use basis to maintain objectivity and reduce the likelihood of personal bias. The offenders were selected and analyzed in three respective groups of thirty, thirty and twenty-five individuals. This was done to avoid the bias that might have arrived from taking large samples just to have the statistics favor the hypothesis.

The results are as follows:

1) In the first group of thirty offenders, 70% committed their crimes during their respective peak sex period.

2) In the second group of thirty offenders, 77% committed their offenses during their respective peak sex period.

3) In the final group of twenty-five offenders, 72% committed their offenses during their respective peak sex period.

4) Consolidating the data of the three groups, 73% of them committed their sex crimes during their respective peak sex period.

This clearly illustrates that individuals are more likely to commit sex crimes during their respective peak sex period. It further illustrates the overpowering influence of the preprogrammed desire or instinct to propagate. Propagation is designed to occur irrespective of our attempts to legislate sexual activity.

Data on Offenders:

1) Ninety-four percent of the offenders were male and six percent were female. This illustrates that males have a far tougher time managing the instinct to propagate than females.

2) The ages of the sex offenders ranged from fifteen to sixty-seven years old. This suggests that the instinct to propagate starts to be overpowering for males at about age fifteen and remains active late into adulthood.

Data on Victims:

1) Eighty-five percent of the victims were female and fifteen percent were male. Thus, females are the more likely targets for sex offenses.

2) The victims' ages ranged from infant to forty-five years old. Thus, there is practically no age group that is exempt from sex crimes.

Female Victims:

1) 8% were 6 years old and younger

2) 27% were between 7 and 12 years old

3) 29% were between 13 and 15 years old

4) 11% were between 16 and 20 years old

5) 25% were 21 and older

Based upon this study, females between the ages of seven and fifteen years old are the most likely victims of sex crimes. Conversations with professionals that provide counseling for victims of sexual assault revealed that not all of the illegal sexual advances were undesired. This suggests that some of the victims may have been at the effect of their peak sex period. In any event, the peak sex period technology can be very useful in curtailing sex offenses by:

1) Raising the individual awareness of the powerful influence of the instinct to propagate and when it is at its most influential point.

2) Informing potential victims when they are likely to find themselves in uncontrollable sexual situations, and with whom.

3) Informing potential offenders when they will most likely be under the influence of the instinct to propagate. This provides them with the means to avoid personal situations that might result in illegal sexual encounters.

4) Identifying and/or catching offenders that have managed to elude discovery. Their illicit

actions and behavior are more recognizable during their respective peak sex period.

The summary data of the study has been included for review in Exhibit A. The intent of this study is only to illuminate a key physical factor that contributes to sexual assault. Though there are other numerous and varied circumstantial and/or psychological factors that are also major contributors to sexual assault, without this physical factor, sex would not exist and neither would sexual assault.

Another huge factor that contributes to male sexual assault of women is how men are taught to relate to women. Men learn how to relate to women primarily from other men. Men learn from men that being dominant is what it is to be truly a man and women are the property of men to be used as they choose. Sexual assault occurs as a result of individuals selecting other individuals they can dominate, and/or as a result of individuals doing what they wish with others they perceived to be property. Once upon a time, and still in some societies today, this was the accepted way of men relating to women. However, in our society today this relationship is not accepted. Women have individual rights that give them control over their bodies, and it is against the law to violate these rights. Many men are having to learn to relate to women appropriately and newly the hard way. That is, by going through the rigors of what it is to be convicted as a sex offender. There is a much easier way for men to learn to relate to women appropriately: **learn from women how to relate to women and not from other men!**

EXHIBIT A
SEX OFFENDER ANALYSIS

One Hundred Percent (85ct)											
Seventy-three Percent In Peak Period (62ct)							Twenty-Seven Percent Outside OF Peak Period (23ct)				
Low	Moderate	High	Highest	High	Moderate	Low	One Month After Peak	Two Months After Peak	None Peak Median	Two Months Before Peak	One Month Before Peak
10ct / 12%	13ct / 15%	4ct / 5%	1ct / 1%	7ct / 8%	18ct / 21%	9ct / 11%	1ct / 1%	8ct / 9.5%	8ct / 9.5%	1ct / 1%	5ct / 6%

Chapter 7

Astrology and the Peak Sex Period

This is an opportunity to become more familiar with the impact the peak sex period has on your behavior and relationships. You will gain insight into what determines the degree of aggressiveness and romanticism of a prospective mate. You will discover that you can or do have a say in how you are romanced. If you are an astrology enthusiast, you will find this application of the peak sex period especially interesting.

With respect to companionship and marriage, astrology recommends the pairing of select astrological signs. For example, the most compatible mates for someone born under the sign of Aries are individuals born either under the sign of Leo or Sagittarius. Each astrological sign has at least two recommended alternate signs for mates. Though the recommendations are based on the individual's time of birth, place on earth at birth and the positions of astrological bodies at birth; the recommendations, if sound, have to somehow include or take into consideration the fundamental biological nature of what it is to be a human being. To this end, it was deemed valuable to find out how the peak sex periods of the astrological signs and the recommended astrological mates matched up.

A chart depicting the peak sex periods of the astrological signs and their recommended companions is presented below. A surprising note is that the peak sex period patterns of the twelve astrological signs are the same for the top two recommended mates. Neither sign is matched such that their peak sex period is a direct match or correlate with the recommended companions' sign, which would make available very high peaks and lows in sexual energy between the couple. Remember, it is the period of low sexual energy that provides a clearing for relationships to end. The likelihood of undesirable relationship issues increases with increased periods of minimal sexual desire or energy.

The peak sex periods of the signs are, instead, positioned to moderately sexually influence the behavior of the couples for eleven of the twelve months, with one month left for no heightened reproductive or sexual influence. Here the emphasis is companionship and not great sex. The sexual roles within the companionship or relationship changes as each person moves through their respective peak sex period. When one person is at the highest point of sexual desire, the other is at the lowest. This puts the person at the highest point of sexual desire in the position of being the sexual aggressor and the other in the position of being the sexually pursued or prey. The roles reverse as the individuals move through their respective peak sex periods. Thus, providing equality relative to sexual aggressiveness.

Using the sign of Aries as a model for each of the other signs, let us assume that Aries has just began her peak sex period and has just met Leo, a prospective mate. The peak sex period of Aries starts four months prior to Leo's, which puts her in the position of the sexual aggressor or romantic. As a result, Aries initiates the relationship with Leo through romantic gestures and actions, and starts the sexual seduction of Leo. Aries will occur to Leo as an aggressive or sexually aggressive female. If Aries is modest and/or adheres to culturally acceptable sexual behavior for women, her seductive actions will consist of numerous and persistent sexually suggestive flirtations until she becomes irresistibly sexually tempting to Leo. If Aries is uninhibited, her seductive actions and activities will be more overt and even provocative. Leo will experience and know Aries as a very aggressive woman who goes to almost any length to get what she desires and wants.

Leo will most be at the effect of the sexual seduction of Aries beginning at or near his birthday in July. As Leo approaches the highest point of his peak cycle in October, Aries approaches her lowest point. Similar to a relay race, the baton of sexual aggressor is passed from Aries to Leo. Come October, Aries has little or no interest in sexual activity and must be seduced by Leo, who does not mind at all because he is at the highest point of sexual desire. Leo vigorously pursues Aries sexually through November and the pursuit starts to noticeably diminish in December, and winds down in January. February is the month of mutually low sexual desire for the couple. In March, the sexual cycle begins anew.

The aggressor/romantic role of Aries would be the same if the genders were reversed. Gender does not determine the aggressor/romantic. The aggressor/romantic is determined by who first entered their peak sex period at the inception of the relationship. However, a key difference would be a greater expression of sexual aggression by the male. This is due primarily to the fact that males are given greater permission for sexually aggressive behavior in our society.

Let us look at the most likely sexual relationship between Aries and Sagittarius, her alternate compatible sign. Assuming they met at the beginning of Sagittarius' peak sex period, Sagittarius would be the aggressor/romantic in this relationship. Aries will likely experience being heavily romanced by Sagittarius. Sagittarius is likely to be very generous towards Aries and endow her with gifts, entertainment and other material gestures symbolizing his affection for her. This is all done to win her favor and sexually seduce her. Aries will likely enjoy and treasure this royal treatment by Sagittarius. A celebrity marriage that clearly demonstrated this romantic behavior was the marriage between Richard Burton, a Scorpio, and Elizabeth Taylor, a Pisces. As depicted in the Chart, the Scorpio and Pisces relationship is a direct correlate of the Sagittarius and Aries relationship in regards to the peak sex period. In this Scorpio/Pisces relationship,

Richard Burton was famous for the expensive gifts of gems he gave to Elizabeth Taylor.

Back to the Sagittarius/Aries relationship, Sagittarius will likely occur to Aries as the person who is driving or running the relationship because of the sexual aggressive behavior of Sagittarius, and Sagittarius will experience himself as head of the relationship or the household. This form of relationship feeds the reputed male ego and provides the **"in-charge-male"** that some females desire. They are out to mate or be sexually active and will go to great lengths to achieve this. Eliminating the effects of culture and other synthetic influences, the "in-charge-male", during his peak sex period, will go to great lengths to figure out what his female partner wants and desires, and will do whatever he can to make her happy during this period. It is no wonder that females enjoy this type of male. Aries, in this relationship, will occur as passive rather than aggressive.

Once the baton of sexual aggressor is passed from Sagittarius to Aries during the first half of Aries' peak sex period, Sagittarius is still likely to experience himself as the person in charge, though he is now being sexually pursued by Aries. The psychological role of being in charge is established at the inception of the relationship and will likely thrive for the duration of the relationship. Aries will likely experience herself as sexually uninhibited as a result of the clearing for sex provided by the prior sexual aggression of Sagittarius. Sagittarius is sexually stimulated and seduced by the uninhibited sexual expressions of Aries throughout the duration of Aries' peak sex period. The ego of Sagittarius will likely attribute Aries' sexually aggressive behavior to his male prowess. In the meantime, Aries will experience herself as the person in charge, though she may not openly express it, because sex is happening consistent with her desire. In the Sagittarius/Aries relationship, the month of mutual minimal sexual desire is October. The cycle for the couple begins newly in November.

Tip: It is useful to chart your individual relationship according to your and your mate's respective peak sex periods, as was done here for the astrological signs. It will provide valuable insight into when your personal behavior and the behavior of your mate will be changing as a result of influences of the peak sex period. Also remember that selecting an aggressive or passive mate is simply a matter of selecting someone whose peak sex period occurs before or after yours. An aggressive and very romantic mate will be one whose peak sex period starts before yours. A passive mate will be one whose peak sex period starts after yours. Many females and males have looked at the mates of friends and others and have wondered why their mate is not as romantic and generous as their friends' mates. The answer lies to a large degree in whether their mate was on the aggressive or passive side of her/his peak sex period at the beginning of the relationship. Remember, the psychological roles established at the inception of the relationship will likely last for the duration of the relationship. Once the psychological roles are established at the initiation of the relationship, they are tough to alter or adjust later.

In conclusion, simply knowing someone's zodiac sign tells you more about her/his sexual behavior than she/he would probably like you to know. On the other side of the coin, someone who knows your zodiac sign knows more about your sexual behavior than you might want her/him to know. A table of the compatible zodiac signs has been included below for your convenience. The *italicized zodiac signs* are the two best recommended for companionship and are depicted in the Chart of Peak Sex Periods of Astrological Signs.

<u>Table of Compatible Signs</u>

Aries – *Sagittarius and Leo*; Aquarius

Taurus – *Capricorn and Virgo*; Cancer

Gemini – *Aquarius, and Libra*

Cancer – *Pisces and Scorpio*; Taurus

Leo – *Aries and Sagittarius*

Virgo – *Taurus and Capricorn*; Pisces

Libra – *Gemini and Aquarius*; Capricorn

Scorpio – *Cancer and Pisces*

Sagittarius – *Leo and Aries*; Sagittarius

Capricorn – *Virgo and Taurus*; Libra

Aquarius – *Libra and Gemini*; Aries

Pisces – *Scorpio and Cancer*; Virgo

CHART
Peak Sex Periods of Astrological Signs

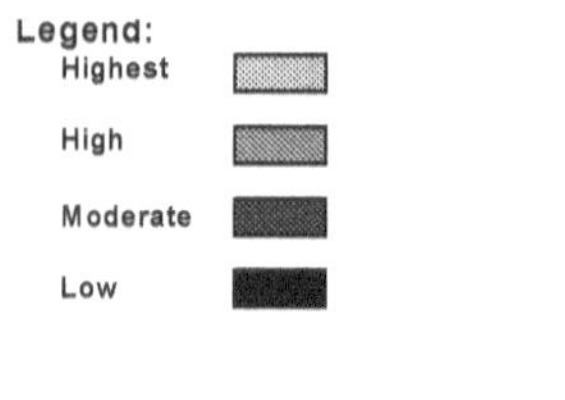

ARIES
March 21 through April 20

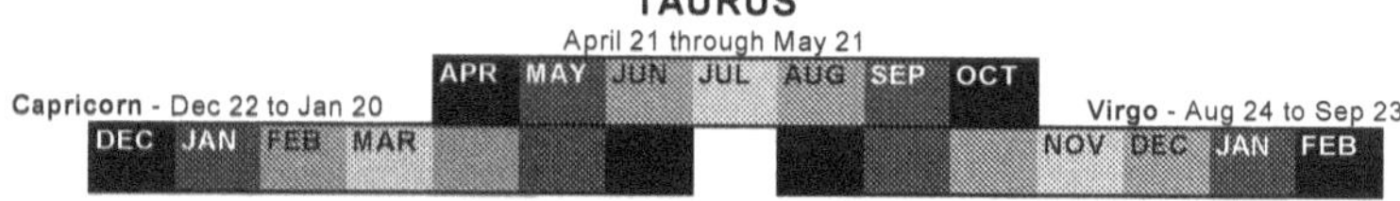

TAURUS
April 21 through May 21

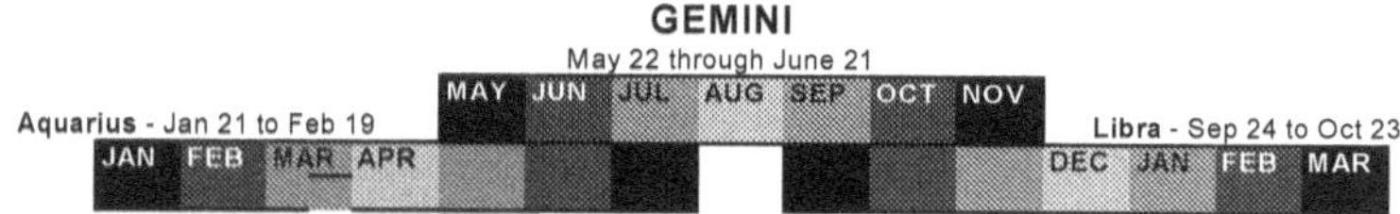

GEMINI
May 22 through June 21

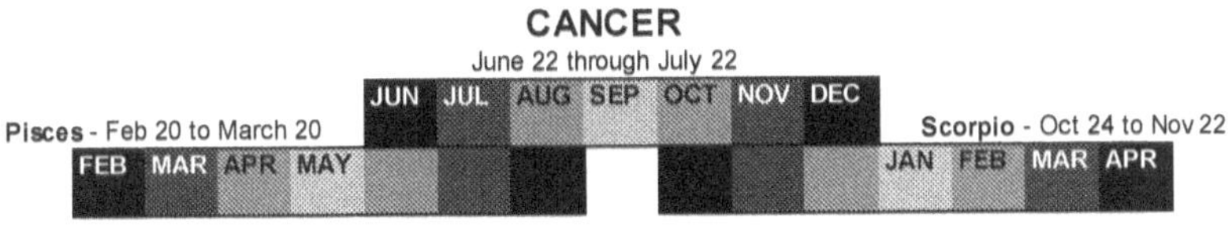
CANCER
June 22 through July 22
JUN JUL AUG SEP OCT NOV DEC
Pisces - Feb 20 to March 20
FEB MAR APR MAY
Scorpio - Oct 24 to Nov 22
JAN FEB MAR APR

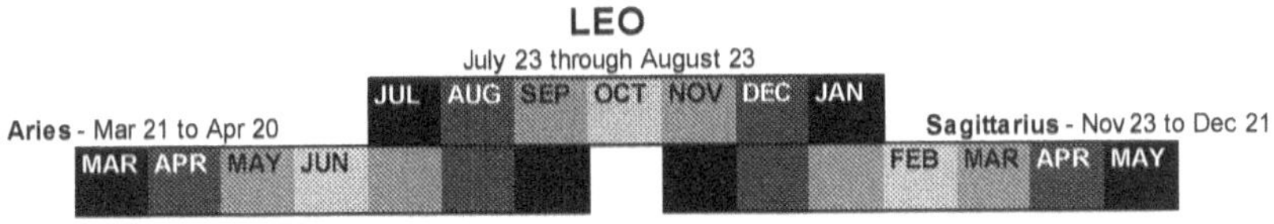
LEO
July 23 through August 23
JUL AUG SEP OCT NOV DEC JAN
Aries - Mar 21 to Apr 20
MAR APR MAY JUN
Sagittarius - Nov 23 to Dec 21
FEB MAR APR MAY

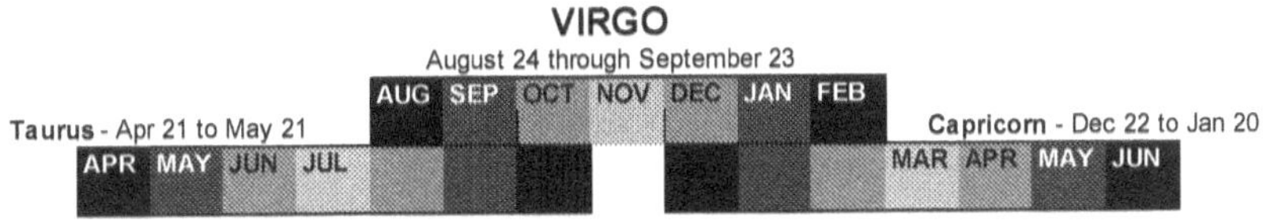
VIRGO
August 24 through September 23
AUG SEP OCT NOV DEC JAN FEB
Taurus - Apr 21 to May 21
APR MAY JUN JUL
Capricorn - Dec 22 to Jan 20
MAR APR MAY JUN

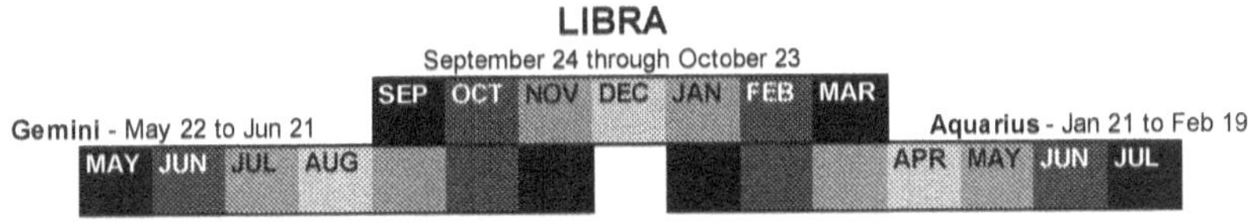
LIBRA
September 24 through October 23
SEP OCT NOV DEC JAN FEB MAR
Gemini - May 22 to Jun 21
MAY JUN JUL AUG
Aquarius - Jan 21 to Feb 19
APR MAY JUN JUL

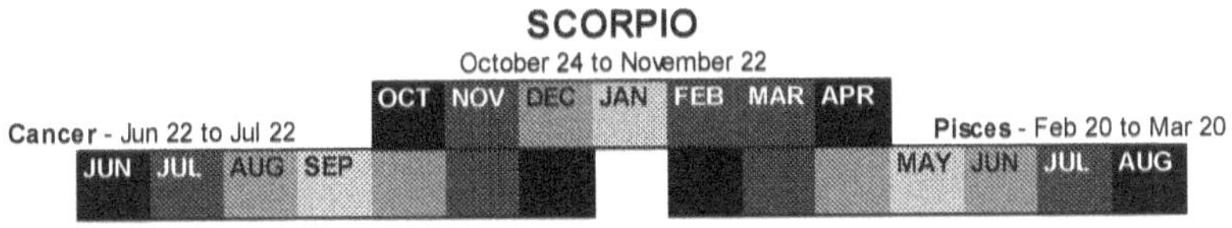
SCORPIO
October 24 to November 22
OCT NOV DEC JAN FEB MAR APR
Cancer - Jun 22 to Jul 22
JUN JUL AUG SEP
Pisces - Feb 20 to Mar 20
MAY JUN JUL AUG

SAGITTARIUS
November 23 through December 21

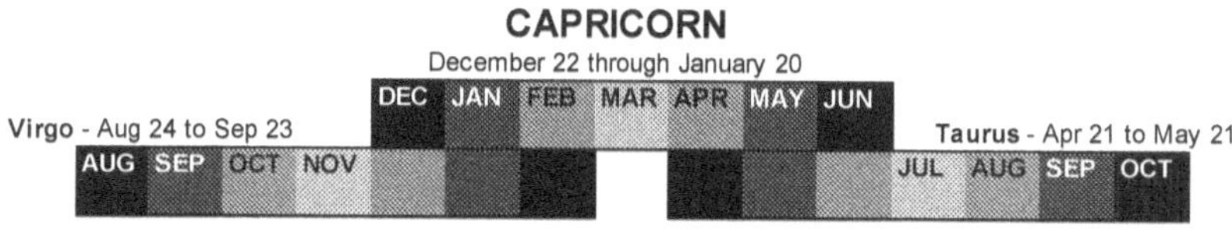

CAPRICORN
December 22 through January 20

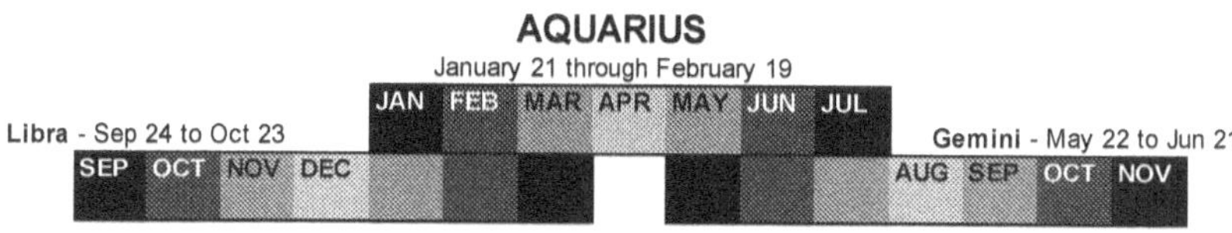

AQUARIUS
January 21 through February 19

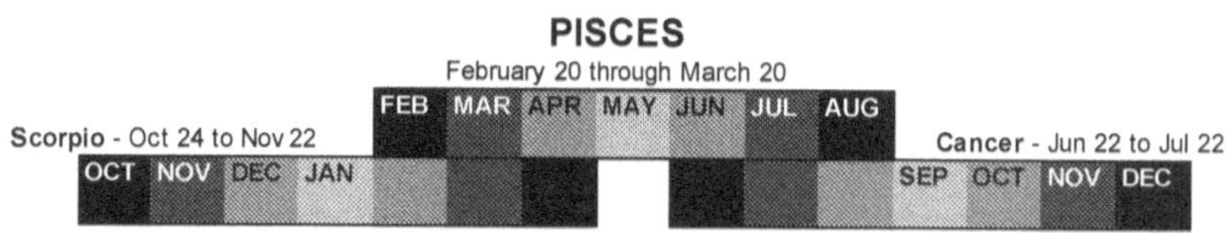

PISCES
February 20 through March 20

Chapter 8

Bio-Bonding of Females and Males

This is another illustration of the effects of bodily chemistry on your behavior and actions. Additionally, one of the simplest and most effortless means of managing the existence of intimate relationships and resolving conflicts within a relationship is presented here.

Since we are in a discussion about the biological influences on female/male relationships, there is one more that warrants inclusion. It is bio-bonding which is more commonly called kissing. The mouth is the central pleasure center of the body. No other part of the body generates the personal experience of pleasure more often and more abundantly. Humans as well as many other animals use the touching of mouths and/or touching another with the tongue to express affection and acceptance of one another.

The touching of mouths or kissing is an attempt to share one's most pleasurable experience with another. The recipient of a kiss, whether kissed on the cheek, lips, mouth or hand, almost always is left with an experience of being contributed to, appreciated, acknowledged, known and/or loved.

One of the first things we do to begin or formalize a relationship is kiss. Kissing is a significant component of weddings. The kissing of the bride symbolizes the final ceremonial bonding of the new husband and wife as "one." Kissing is a process of bonding chemically to one's mate, the process of physically becoming one with one's mate. In addition, kissing assists in the selection of a chemically compatible mate for the conception of children.

In regards to relationships, we instinctually know there is no such thing as an innocent kiss. We instinctively know that our mate chemically bonds to another person that she/he kisses, and our upset and jealousy are natural reactions to the chance of losing our mate to another. If your mate kisses someone else, the appropriate and immediate action is to kiss your mate as soon as possible to reestablish your chemical bond with your mate. This also removes the chemical traces of the would-be intruder. Many people naturally do this. However, it seems as if more people react and do the opposite. They react or get upset and refuse to kiss their mate, which generates more separation between themselves and their mate. They romanticize that they are punishing their mate for her/his actions. Contrary to their intent, they are actually killing off the relationship. The further separation causes a breach in their chemical bonding, which increases the likelihood of the relationship failing. What there is to remember here is that regular kissing maintains and nurtures the relationship, and no kissing will most likely result in the demise of the relationship.

Individuals that are committed to being independent, in control and/or avoiding the dominance of another usually avoid kissing as much as possible. They instinctively know that kissing is dangerous to their commitment to being separate, since it promotes oneness rather than separateness.

Kissing greatly assists in the resolution of problems within the relationship. There was an adage that was once widely used as an antidote for resolving most relationship problems. The adage is "kiss and make up." This adage is the best possible beginning for resolving relationship issues and problems. First you kiss and then you begin to work out the problems or make up. Kissing restores the chemical bonding and reestablishes the "oneness" between you and your mate. With "oneness" restored, each of you has less attention on individual wants and desires. Each of you is naturally more concerned with what works best for the "couple" or the relationship. As a result, problems are efficiently and effectively worked out inside of the "oneness" of the couple; rather than each individual struggling to work out problems as two biologically unrelated individuals.

Today, this adage is forgotten and couples attempt to work out issues by first resolving the issue and then kissing. If you do this, you are doing the reverse of what works best. Working out relationship issues as individuals is almost certain to result in a relationship disaster. An individual is only interested in that which supports and ensures the survival of itself as an individual, and could care less about another or the relationship. The key to remember here is that first you kiss and then you work on the issues, and never reverse the order.

All the kissing that was done to initiate and establish the relationship is required to maintain and nurture the growth of the relationship. So, be generous with the kissing of each other.

Chapter 9

The Male Menopause Myth

This is the opportunity to examine another unrecognized sexual biorhythm and dispel the myth of male menopause. The outcomes are the wherewithal to make better decisions in selecting lifelong mates and better management of female/male relationships.

It is readily observable and is the general consensus that men go through a unique behavioral period, which begins in their late thirties and continues throughout their forties and sometimes fifties. As a result of a lack of understanding of this unique period for men, it has been referred to as men's "midlife crisis." Some individuals misinterpret it as "male menopause," relating it to the menopausal cycle of women. That which men go through during this unique male period is neither a crisis nor menopause.

Biologically, males are not born with all the sperm, genetic coding, they will ever possess. There is a divine purpose for this. Anything that is whole, complete and lacking nothing, as are females in this case, cannot be added to. For example: You cannot add more water to a glass that is already full of water; you can only add more water if the glass is not full. Males are not full genetically and thus, can be contributed to genetically.

As a simple review of human sexual biology, each human cell contains forty-six chromosomes. From a sexual standpoint, normal females have forty-four regular chromosomes plus two X-sex chromosomes; and normal males have forty-four regular chromosomes plus one X- and one Y-sex chromosome, as depicted in Illustration A below. Thus, the X- and Y-chromosomes are what distinguishes female from male.

If a normal female egg, X-bearing, is fertilized by an X-bearing normal male sperm, an "XX" chromosome combination is the result; the offspring is female. The X-bearing sperm results in a complete genetic package that results in all of the female eggs being produced.

When a normal female egg, X-bearing, is fertilized by a Y-bearing normal male sperm, an "XY" chromosome combination is the result; the offspring is male. The Y-bearing sperm results in an incomplete genetic package and the male sex organs are produced. The Y-chromosome can be thought of as an X-chromosome that is missing a part of itself. It is this male genetic "missing" or incomplete genetic package that allows for a species to be contributed to genetically. It is through the male of the species that evolution within the species occurs. The environment, world and universe are in a state of perpetual change. The male is that part of the species that senses this perpetual change and provides the genetic evolutionary enhancements to ensure the survival and/or growth of the species.

Illustration A

Evolution of a species is accomplished through the male of the species. If significant and drastic changes occurred in a species' environment, the species would cease to exist if there were no access to sensing and adjusting to the change. The ancients understood this, and the appropriate emphasis was put on men to be out in the world so that they may be exposed to the perpetual change.

The male can be likened to an unripe fruit that requires time to ripen or mature to the fullness of its essence. In almost every aspect of nature, the male has to demonstrate that he has indeed matured to the fullness of his essence. That is, he has lived and experienced life long enough to have adequately sampled his environment, and has sufficiently incorporated the environmental conditions genetically within his seed. Males then compete for the privilege to father the next generation of the species. The male that has best incorporated the environmental conditions genetically is usually the strongest and the victor in the competition for fathering the next generation. In some animal societies, wolves for example, only the alpha female and alpha male mate. These animal societies take advantage of the best that both genders have to offer.

The ancients recognized the male as the unripe fruit of the culture/species that must be nurtured and used only when it was fully ripe or mature. They were wise in that they recognized the male reached the peak of maturity when he entered or neared his forties. The key ingredients to male maturation are time and experience. Sufficient time is required for the male to be exposed to the environment in order to sufficiently sample and genetically incorporate the environmental changes. Experience is the method by which the environmental sampling takes place. The more varied and numerous the male experiences, the more efficient and effective the sampling process. Thus, it is important that the male have full access to the environment and the opportunity to explore and experience the environment.

To see this genetic coding at work in building a people, all that is needed is to return to the book of Genesis and the life of Abraham. Here, God is building a people through the genetic coding of Abraham and his wife Sarah. In Genesis 17:16 God says to Abraham:

> **"And I will bless her, and give thee a son also of her: yea, I will bless her, and she shall be *a mother* of nations; kings of people shall be of her."**

Here, God is referring to the birth of Isaac. It is Isaac that is to be God's masterpiece. It took Abraham a hundred years to ripen to a point he was useful by God to father kings. This wisdom into the maturation of the male was with the descendants of Abraham, as depicted in Genesis 37:3:

"Now Israel loved Joseph more than all his Children, because he was the son of his old age: and he made him a coat of many colours."

In cultures where the building of the people/species was of central importance, men did not enter into marriage until they were approximately forty-five years old. It was this approximate age that all their apprenticeships were complete and they had come into their own wealth, symbols of their genetic maturity. Their wives were fifteen or more years younger than them, the perfect combination for conceiving the next generation.

Our society, on the other hand, legislates when men are mature. Herein lie the problems many females find with men. We say that men are mature when they reach eighteen or twenty-one years of age. This is analogous to an apple grower attempting to legislate at what time all the apples will be mature enough to harvest. The apple grower knows that not all trees produce ripe fruit at the exact same time and not all fruit of a single tree ripen at the exact same time. The apple grower has the wisdom to select the ripe fruit from each tree and leave the rest to ripen. If we exercised the wisdom of an apple grower, a number of the current-day complaints about men would be eliminated.

A source of anger and upsets is unfulfilled expectations. We expect an unripe man, "boy toy," to behave in the same manner as a ripe man in regards to marriage and intimate relationships. We get upset when he does not fulfill our expectations of him. An unripe fruit will never taste as good as a fruit that is fully ripened. If we can readily discern this about fruit, it is insanity to expect something different from men.

When men reach the peak of ripeness or maturity, the natural inclination to mate or sow the seed is irresistible. Since many men in our society marry in their teens and twenties, when they are not fully mature, a problem arises when they reach their peak of ripeness. He naturally starts to look for a fertile field in which to plant his mature seed. This happens to most men when they reach their late thirties and forties. His wife who is about the same age as he may be entering menopause and/or desire not to have additional children. Thus, there is a non-matching of the biological reproductive rhythms when the married couple are of the same age. When the husband is entering his peak season of ripeness in terms of reproduction, his wife is leaving her period of reproduction.

The fully ripened husband will desire or be naturally pulled to have children even though his wife may no longer have such desires. As a result, he will look for another woman to be the field in which to plant his mature seed. Younger females will occur more attractive to him because of his innate perception of them being more fertile than older women. Without strong cultural influences to remain married and/or the ability to live as their word, many men will divorce, remarry and/or have children out of wedlock; oftentimes with a younger female. Men who find themselves at the effect of this powerful and irresistible natural drive to propagate are frowned upon in our society and deemed to have psychological issues. This is not a male psychological problem. It is just "Species" getting its job done. Remember the phrases "it is easier to ride the horse in the direction it is going" or "never drink a wine before its time." The ancients were wise in only putting the mature male into marriage. We are not so wise, and have to deal with the resulting marital and relationship issues from unmatched female and male biological reproductive rhythms.

The biological reproductive rhythms of females and males are depicted below in Illustration B. Since individuals began puberty at different times and for the sake of simplicity, the female and male sexual maturity rates are assumed to be the same through puberty. Notice, we are not designed to be reproductively active our entire lives. Our first period of life as children is where we are free of the natural mandate to support the survival of the species, or free to be self-expressed. Similar to being involuntarily drafted into the military, we are drafted into the service of "species" and sexual maturity begins. Once we reach sexual maturity, the central thrust of our lives is the continuance of the species or reproduction. Females leave this period of reproductive service prior to males, and their exit is initiated by what is termed as menopause. Once menopause is complete for females, they are again free of the reproductive mandates of "species" and regain the freedom to be self-expressed. Males, on the other hand, leave sexual maturity and enter a continued reproductive service cycle, genetic maturity. Relative to females, males regain the freedom to be self-expressed much later in life. Because females leave the reproductive service of "species" much sooner than males, females are more available for the objective governance of their respective cultures and societies than males. Few cultures and/or societies have taken advantage of this female freedom to be self-expressed while men are still in the reproductive service of "species."

<u>Illustration B</u>

Female and Male Reproductive Life Cycles

Free to be Self-Expressed	Beginning of Puberty	*FEMALE* Sexual Maturity	*FEMALE* Menopause	Regained freedom to be Self-Expressed

Free to be Self-Expressed	Beginning of Puberty	*MALE* Sexual Maturity	*MALE* Genetic Maturity	Regained freedom to be Self-Expressed

In regards to attraction, now it is understandable why many women consider middle-age men attractive. It is the middle-aged man's genetic maturity and symbols of genetic maturity that are women's primary innate attractions to men, during women's tenure of reproductive service. During men's tenure of reproductive service, men's innate central attractions to women are women's fertility and symbols of fertility.

In regards to female/male relationships, acknowledge the truth about the male fruit you are in a relationship with. Understand that his behavior and actions are due in part to his degree of ripeness. We cannot legislate when men are ripe. It does not work that way. Ripe is different for each man. Each man has different requirements in regards to time and varied experiences to reach his peak of genetic maturity. Generally speaking, *if the apple of your eye is less than thirty-years old, he is not yet ripe!*

NOTES

NOTES

NOTES

NOTES

NOTES

Henry H. Bowens
hhbowens@aol.com

Abbreviated Biography

MBA, Accounting-Finance Concentration, Washington University, St. Louis, Missouri, 1977; **BBA**, Accounting, Georgia State University, Atlanta, Georgia, 1975. Administrative and Financial Officers: Business and government for seventeen years.

Oracle Relationships Consultants, Owner: Specializing in personal relationship coaching, and customized business and personal relationship seminars and workshops.

Employed and served in the capacity of senior program leader and program leader trainer for more than fifteen years. Led programs for several renowned human development companies. Led programs to and coached more than ten thousand participants. The programs improved and provided breakthroughs in individuals' experience and satisfaction of living life. The programs led include, but are not limited to, the following topics: Sex, Money, Relationships, Time Management, Increasing Individual Effectiveness, Managing Physical Fitness and Well-Being, Managing the Realization of Commitments, Managing Problems and Breakdowns, and Creating New Paradigms for Living.

www.ingramcontent.com/pod-product-compliance
Lightning Source LLC
Chambersburg PA
CBHW031309060726
47590CB00003B/1123